Business Tax
(Finance Act 2023)

Workbook

for assessments from 29 January 2024

Aubrey Penning
Bob Thomas

Published by Osborne Books Limited
Tel 01905 748071
Email books@osbornebooks.co.uk
Website www.osbornebooks.co.uk

Design by Laura Ingham

Printed by CPI Group (UK) Limited, Croydon, CR0 4YY, on environmentally friendly, acid-free paper from managed forests.

British Library Cataloguing in Publication Data
A catalogue record for this book is available from the British Library

ISBN 978-1-911681-08-3

Contents

Introduction

Chapter activities

Answers to chapter activities

Practice assessments

Answers to practice assessments

Introduction

Qualifications covered

This book has been written specifically to cover the Unit 'Business Tax' which is optional for the following qualifications:

AAT Level 4 Diploma in Professional Accounting

AAT Diploma in Professional Accounting – SCQF Level 8

This book contains Chapter Activities which provide extra practice material in addition to the activities included in the Osborne Books Tutorial text, and Practice Assessments to prepare the student for the computer based assessments. The latter are based directly on the structure, style and content of the sample assessment material provided by the AAT at www.aat.org.uk.

Suggested answers to the Chapter Activities and Practice Assessments are set out in this book.

Osborne Study and Revision Materials

Additional materials, tailored to the needs of students studying this unit and revising for the assessment, include:

- **Tutorials:** paperback books with practice activities
- **Student Zone:** access to Osborne Books online resources
- **Osborne Books App:** Osborne Books ebooks for mobiles and tablets

Visit www.osbornebooks.co.uk for details of study and revision resources and access to online material.

Exams, Finance Acts and tax years

This book has been designed to include guidance and exercises based on Tax Year 2023/24 (Finance Act 2023). We understand that the AAT plans to assess this legislation from 29 January 2024 to January 2025. Tutors and students are advised to check the dates with the AAT and ensure that they sit the correct computer based assessment.

Chapter activities

1   Introduction to business taxation

1.1   Which of the following statements are true and which are false?

		True	False
(a)	A self-employed taxpayer must pay Class 2 NIC, unless the 'small profits threshold' applies		
(b)	Class 4 NIC is payable by the self-employed only when drawings are over £12,570		
(c)	Class 4 NIC is payable by the self-employed when profits are over £12,570		
(d)	Class 4 NIC is paid at the same time as Income Tax under self-assessment		
(e)	Class 4 NIC is payable at 2% on profits over £50,270		

1.2   Using the following table, insert the details and dates relating to online returns and payment of tax.

	Period return relates to	**Latest return submission date**	**Latest tax payment date**
Corporation Tax			
Income Tax			

Select from the following:

- Tax year
- Financial year
- 12 months after end of tax year
- 12 months after end of Chargeable Accounting Period
- 9 months and one day after end of Chargeable Accounting Period
- 12 months after end of period that accounts are based on

- Chargeable Accounting Period
- 31 January following tax year
- 31 October following tax year

1.3

    (a)   A taxpayer has self-employed income of £60,000 for the tax year 2023/24. The amount chargeable to NIC at 9% would be:

    £ [   ]

    (b)   A taxpayer has self-employed income of £48,000 for the tax year 2023/24. The amount of total Class 4 NIC payable would be:

    £ [   ]

1.4   State whether each of the following is true or false.

		True	False
(a)	A self-employed individual's tax records relating to his business for 2023/24 need to be kept until 31 January 2030, or longer if an investigation is being carried out		
(b)	HMRC has a right to visit premises to inspect records		
(c)	Accountants must normally follow the rules of confidentiality, but there are exceptions		
(d)	Where a practitioner has knowledge or suspicion that his client is money laundering, then he has a duty to inform the relevant person or authority		
(e)	The AAT Code of Professional Ethics applies to AAT members, but not to AAT students		
(f)	When an accountant is advising a client, the greatest duty of care is to HMRC		

1.5   State the final submission dates for tax returns for the following businesses.

A sole trader with accounts made up to 31 March 2024	
A limited company with accounts made up to 31 December 2023	

2   Corporation Tax – trading profits

2.1   A limited company has the income and expenses as shown in the following table recorded in its statement of profit or loss. In order to calculate the adjusted trading profit, some items need to be added and some deducted from the net profit. Some items do not require any adjustment.

Analyse the income and expenses, by ticking the appropriate columns in the table.

	Add to net profit	Deduct from net profit	No adjustment required
Depreciation			
Discount received			
Directors' salaries			
Dividends received			
Rent receivable			
Rent payable			
Interest payable			
Advertising costs			
Entertaining customers			

2.2   River Limited has the following summarised statement of profit or loss.

	£	£
Sales		120,000
less cost of sales		35,000
gross profit		85,000
add gain on sale of non-current asset		12,000
		97,000
less expenses:		
administration expenses	18,000	
depreciation	13,000	
charitable payments (QCD)	2,000	
entertaining staff	5,000	
vehicle expenses	22,000	
		60,000
Net profit		37,000

Select the adjusted trading profit (before capital allowances) from the following:

(a)	£57,000	
(b)	£45,000	
(c)	£40,000	
(d)	£34,000	
(e)	£37,000	
(f)	£38,000	

2.3   State whether each of the following statements regarding limited companies is true or false.

		True	False
(a)	The basis of assessment for trading profits is the tax adjusted trading profits of the Chargeable Accounting Period, prepared on an accruals basis		
(b)	Lease rental payments for cars are never allowable as they are deemed to be capital expenditure		
(c)	Interest payable on trade loans is not allowable		
(d)	If a loan to an employee is written off, the amount is not an allowable deduction		
(e)	Donations to political parties are an allowable expense		
(f)	Employers' National Insurance Contributions are not an allowable deduction as they are effectively a form of taxation		
(g)	Employees' parking fines incurred while on business are an allowable deduction		

2.4   If an accounting period is longer than 12 months, which of the following statements shows the correct approach?

(a)	Provided the accounting period is not more than 18 months long, the whole period can form one Chargeable Accounting Period	
(b)	The capital allowances are calculated for the long accounting period and deducted from the adjusted trading profits for the long accounting period. This is then time-apportioned into two Chargeable Accounting Periods	
(c)	It is illegal to prepare accounts for a limited company for more than 12 months, so the problem does not arise	
(d)	The trading profits for the long accounting period are time-apportioned into two periods before tax adjustments are carried out to each period's profit. Capital allowances are calculated for the long period and then time-apportioned, before being deducted from each period's adjusted profits	
(e)	The trading profits for the long period are adjusted for tax purposes (before capital allowances), and the result is time-apportioned into two Chargeable Accounting Periods. Separate capital allowance computations are carried out for each Chargeable Accounting Period, and then deducted from each of the adjusted trading profits	

2.5   A limited company has the following tax-adjusted results for years to 31 December 2022 and 2023:

	2022	2023
Trading Income	£50,000	£0
Income from Investments	£18,000	£15,000
Chargeable Gains	£0	£10,000

The company made a trading loss in 2023 of £81,000.

The company is continuing to trade.

What is the maximum amount of loss that could be set against the taxable total profits for 2022?

(a)	£56,000	
(b)	£68,000	
(c)	£50,000	
(d)	£66,000	
(e)	£0	

3   Corporation Tax – capital allowances

3.1   Analyse the following items into those that qualify as plant and machinery for capital allowance purposes (under Corporation Tax) and those that do not, by ticking the appropriate column.

	Qualify	Do not qualify
Car for employee's private use		
Office furniture		
Capital expenditure on software		
Payments for vehicle on operating lease		
Vehicles bought on credit		
Buildings		
Equipment bought through hire purchase		

3.2   A company has a 12-month Chargeable Accounting Period ending on 31/3/2024, with no written down values brought forward for capital allowance purposes. During the period the company purchased:

- A new zero-emission car for £26,000
- A car with emissions of 180 g/km for £22,000
- Second-hand plant for £60,000

Calculate the maximum capital allowances that can be claimed, and insert the figures into the following sentences.

The Full Expensing allowance that can be claimed is £

The AIA that can be claimed is £

The first year allowance that can be claimed at 100% is £

The writing down allowance that can be claimed at 18% is £

The writing down allowance that can be claimed at 6% is £

The total capital allowance that can be claimed is £

3.3   Analyse each of the following capital acquisitions into the relevant possible category (or categories) by ticking the appropriate column.

	AIA (to limit)	Main pool	Special rate pool	100% FYA	Full Expensing FYA
Car emissions of 185 g/km					
Car emissions of 39 g/km					
Machinery					
Zero-emission goods vehicle					
Car emissions of 105 g/km					

3.4   State whether each of the following statements is true or false.

		True	False
(a)	For a CAP of 9 months, the AIA for each acquisition that qualifies would be scaled down to 9/12 of its cost. For example, an asset bought for £20,000 would only be entitled to £15,000 AIA		
(b)	For a CAP of 9 months, any writing down allowance would be scaled down to 9/12 of the equivalent amount for a 12 month period, but first year allowances and balancing allowances would not be affected		
(c)	For a CAP of 9 months, any first year allowance would be scaled down to 9/12 of the equivalent amount for a 12 month period, but writing down allowances and balancing allowances would not be affected		
(d)	For a CAP of 9 months, the annual investment allowance (AIA) limit would be calculated by time-apportionment		
(e)	For a CAP of 9 months, the writing down allowance is unaffected		

3.5 A company has the following information regarding its non-current assets for a 12-month CAP, ending on 31/12/2023.

	£
Written down values brought forward:	
General (main) pool	120,000
Special rate pool	19,000
Additions:	
New machinery (bought April 2023)	60,000
New car for Sales Director (emissions 190 g/km)	35,000
Disposals:	
Machinery (AIA claimed when acquired)	5,000
Sales Director's car (special rate pool)	7,000

Calculate the maximum capital allowances for the CAP.

4 Corporation Tax – chargeable gains

4.1 Select the appropriate disposal proceeds amount to be used in the chargeable gains computation of a limited company by ticking the appropriate column.

	Actual proceeds	Market value	Zero
Sale of asset for £15,000 to Director who owns 80% of shares in company. Market value of asset is £35,000			
Gift of asset to unconnected individual (non-shareholder)			
Sale of asset to company employee (non-shareholder) at below market value			
Destruction of an uninsured asset during fire			
Sale of asset for £15,000 to Director who owns 10% of shares in company. Market value of asset is £35,000			
Shares owned in an unconnected company that have become worthless due to the company's liquidation			

4.2   Penfold Ltd bought 8,000 shares in Tempter Ltd for £19,500 in October 2001. A rights issue of 1 for 40 shares was bought in July 2003 for £1.80 per share. In April 2023, Penfold Ltd sold 6,000 of the shares for £5 per share.

Indexation factors were: October 2001 to July 2003: 0.114; July 2003 to December 2017: 0.534.

What is the gain made on the share disposal?

	No. Shares	Cost £	Indexed Cost £

Proceeds	£
Indexed Cost	£
Gain	£

4.3   Dee Ltd purchased a shop in September 1986 for £560,000. In January 1992 an extension was added at a cost of £300,000.

The shop was sold in June 2023 for £2,250,000.

Required:

Calculate the chargeable gain arising from the disposal of the shop.

The relevant indexation factors are:

September 1986 to December 2017	1.829
January 1992 to December 2017	1.051

4.4   Gee Ltd purchased a building in August 1998 for £500,000. A piece of land was bought in April 2023 for £850,000.

The building was sold in September 2023 for £980,000.

The indexation factor from August 1998 to December 2017 is 0.729.

Required:

(a)   Calculate the chargeable gain arising from the disposal of the building, after making any relevant claims.

(b)   Note how any rollover of the gain could take place in the future.

5 Corporation Tax – calculating the tax

5.1 Different types of losses can be relieved in different ways. From the list below, select at least one rule that can apply to each of the losses stated in the table.

Loss	Rules that can apply
Trading Loss	
Capital Loss	
Rental Loss	

Select from:

(a) Set against current period taxable total profits (TTP), with any unused amount carried forward and set against future taxable total profits (TTP)

(b) Set against chargeable gains of same CAP, with any unused loss set against taxable total profits (TTP) of current period

(c) Set against chargeable gains of same CAP, with any unused loss set against chargeable gains of previous period

(d) Set against current period taxable total profits (TTP), with any unused amount carried forward and set against future chargeable gains

(e) Set against taxable total profits (TTP) of future CAP

(f) Set against chargeable gains of same CAP, with any unused loss set against chargeable gains of following period

5.2 Calculate the Corporation Tax Liability for each of the following unconnected companies.

(a) Company A has an 8 month CAP ending on 31/12/2023 with TTP of £100,000. It has no associated companies.

(b) Company B has a 12 month CAP ending on 31/12/2023 with TTP of £280,000. It has no associated companies.

(c) Company C has a 12 month CAP ending on 31/3/2024 with TTP of £65,000. It has three associated companies.

5.3   State whether each of the following statements is true or false.

		True	False
(a)	Companies must inform HMRC within six months that they have started trading. The penalty for failing to notify is £3,000		
(b)	The flat penalty for failure to submit a Corporation Tax Return on time is £100 for up to three months late and £200 for over three months late. A percentage penalty based on the Corporation Tax can also apply		
(c)	Interest is charged on late payments (including instalments). The interest charged is an allowable deduction against non-trading interest		
(d)	Errors in tax returns caused by a lack of reasonable care can suffer a penalty of between 0% and 50% of the extra tax due		
(e)	Failure to keep records can result in a penalty of £3,000 per Chargeable Accounting Period		
(f)	Errors in tax returns that are both deliberate and concealed are subject to a penalty of up to 100% of the extra tax due		
(g)	Records need to be kept for at least six years from the end of the accounting period		

5.4   Examine the following list of situations where there were errors in company tax returns, and state both the minimum and maximum penalties that would arise as percentages of the additional tax due.

(a)   A manual stock count resulted in an under-statement of inventory and an under-statement of profit. This was due to a page of working papers being mislaid and omitted from the total valuation. When this was discovered by the company accountant, HMRC was immediately notified.

(b)   A company director had used his company credit card to purchase a new car for his wife, who is not an employee. The company accountant was aware of the situation, but he included the amount in the cost of sales expense category, hoping that it would not be discovered. HMRC discovered the anomaly during a routine enquiry.

(c)   A company that ran a chain of restaurants excluded cash receipts from their records entirely. The cash was used to pay bonuses to company directors. When a new firm of accountants was employed, the directors were persuaded to notify HMRC of their concealed activities.

6   Income Tax – trading profits

6.1   From the following factors, tick those that are considered the 'badges of trade' which are used to determine whether an individual is trading.

	Badges of Trade
Reason for acquisition and sale of item(s)	
Whether individual enjoys carrying out the activity	
Whether there is a profit motive	
How long the individual has owned the item(s) before sale	
Whether the individual only sells via computer sites	
Whether any supplementary work is carried out on the item(s) before sale	
Whether the individual considers the activity to be his hobby	
How often the individual carries out similar transactions	
Whether the items bought and sold (the subject matter) are used personally by the individual before sale	

6.2   Analyse the following expenditure of a sole trader into those that are allowable deductions for tax purposes and those that are not, by ticking the appropriate column.

	Allowable expenditure	Non-allowable expenditure
Cost of sales		
Entertaining staff		
Fines for lawbreaking by business owner		
Gifts of food or drink to customers		
Trade bad debts written off		
Salary and NIC of business owner		
Depreciation		
Loss on sale of non-current assets		

6.3   Laura Little is a sole trader. Her business has the following statement of profit or loss:

	£	£
Turnover		1,256,000
Cost of sales		815,400
Gross profit		440,600
Wages and salaries	120,560	
Rent, rates and insurance	51,210	
Repairs to plant	8,615	
Advertising and entertaining	19,535	
Accountancy and legal costs	5,860	
Motor expenses	50,030	
Telephone and office costs	18,050	
Depreciation	22,020	
Other expenses	32,410	328,290
Net Profit		112,310

Notes:

1.   Laura took goods from the business that cost £1,200 and would normally sell for £2,000. The cost is included in cost of sales.

2.   Wages and salaries include: £
        Laura Little   45,000
        Laura's son, who works during the school holidays   28,000

3.   Advertising and entertaining includes: £
        Gifts to customers:
                Bottles of wine costing £12 each   2,400
                400 mouse mats carrying the business's logo   600

4.   Motor expenses include: £
        Delivery van expenses   10,150
        Laura's car expenses (used for business only)   5,900
        Laura's son's car expenses (used only for private use)   3,800

5.   Other expenses include: £
        Cost of staff training   3,150
        Increase in general bad debt provision   2,600

6.   Capital allowances have already been calculated at £10,400

Complete the adjusted trading profits computation.

6.4   Mavis Deacon has a 12-month accounting period ending on 31/3/2024, with no written down values brought forward for capital allowance purposes. In January 2024 she purchased:

- A van with 20% private use for £18,000

- A car with emissions of 100 g/km and 40% private use for £20,000

- Machinery for £30,000

Calculate the maximum capital allowances that can be claimed, and insert the figures into the following sentences.

The AIA that can be claimed is £ [   ]

The single asset pool writing down allowance that can be claimed is £ [   ]

The main rate pool writing down allowance that can be claimed is £ [   ]

The total capital allowance that can be claimed is £ [   ]

The total written down value carried forward is £ [   ]

7 Income Tax – further issues

7.1 An established sole trader has the following tax-adjusted results for the tax years shown:

	2022/23	2023/24
Trading Profits	£20,000	£0
Other Income	£17,000	£28,000

The sole trader incurred a trading loss in 2023/24 of £44,000. The business is continuing.

What is the maximum amount of the loss that could be set against the individual's income for 2022/23?

(a)	£20,000	
(b)	£37,000	
(c)	£44,000	
(d)	£16,000	
(e)	£0	

7.2 Pete and Heather have been in partnership for many years, running a fish smoking business, and sharing profits equally. They have always made their accounts up to 31 December each year.

On 1 September 2023, Ash joined the partnership and the profit sharing ratio was changed to 3:3:2 for Pete, Heather and Ash.

For the year ended 31 December 2023, the trading profit was £120,000.

Using the following table, calculate the division of profits between the partners for the accounting year ended 31 December 2023.

	Total £	Pete £	Heather £	Ash £
1 Jan – 31 August 2023				
1 Sep – 31 Dec 2023				
Total				

7.3   Joe Salt's total Income Tax and Class 4 NIC for 2022/23 has been finalised as £11,600, all relating to his business as a sole trader. He made payments on account of £4,000 on each of 31 January 2023 and 31 July 2023 relating to 2022/23.

Using the following table, calculate the amounts of the payments that he needs to make on 31 January 2024 and 31 July 2024, assuming no claim to reduce payments is made.

		£
Payment on 31 January 2024	Balance of tax and NIC for 2022/23	
	Payment on account for 2023/24	
	Total	
Payment on 31 July 2024	Payment on account for 2023/24	

8   Business disposals and tax planning

8.1   The following statements relate to Business Asset Disposal Relief. State whether each of the statements is true or false.

		True	False
(a)	It is subject to a lifetime limit of £1,000,000 per individual		
(b)	It works by charging the gain at 8%		
(c)	All disposals made by an individual are eligible		
(d)	It can relate to the disposal of shares held in a 'personal trading company'		
(e)	It is subject to a lifetime limit of £100,000,000		
(f)	It works by charging the gain at 10%		
(g)	It effectively uses up the basic rate band so other gains that are not eligible are more likely to be taxed at 20%		

8.2   David and Josie Smith are both higher rate taxpayers. They have recently decided to sell the limited company that they started in 2001. They are the only shareholders, and they each invested £30,000 in ordinary £2 shares at par when the company was founded.

They were both employed by the company, and it traded successfully until June 2023, when they accepted an offer of £18 per share for both shareholdings. They have never claimed Business Asset Disposal Relief previously, and they have no other gains in 2023/24.

Required:

(a)   Explain whether they meet the criteria to claim Business Asset Disposal Relief.

(b)   Calculate the amount of Capital Gains Tax payable each for 2023/24.

8.3 Emma has started a limited company as sole shareholder, and she expects the company to generate profits of between £60,000 and £80,000 per year from April 2023. She already has property income of £15,000 per year, and dividends from investments of £3,000 per year which will continue.

She is considering the implications of extracting profit from her company either as salary or dividends. Complete the following table to summarise the situation.

	Salary	**Dividends**
Personal position:		
Income Tax rates range		
Employees' NIC payable?		
Company position:		
Corporation Tax % saving		
Employers' NIC payable?		

8.4 Brian and Ellen are a married couple. They each own 50% of the ordinary shares in a limited company that Ellen runs.

Brian looks after their two young children. Ellen works full time in the business, and she takes a director's salary of £90,000. The profits for the business are approximately £120,000 per year. Neither Ellen or Brian currently take any dividends, nor have income from any other source.

They are considering reducing Ellen's salary to £60,000, and then paying £15,000 to each of them as dividends.

Explain the impact of the proposal in terms of Income Tax, National Insurance Contributions, and Corporation Tax. You do not need to carry out calculations.

Answers to chapter activities

1 Introduction to business taxation

1.1 **(a)**, **(c)**, **(d)** and **(e)** are true; **(b)** is false.

1.2

	Period return relates to	Latest return submission date	Latest tax payment date
Corporation Tax	Chargeable Accounting Period	12 months after end of period that accounts are based on	9 months and one day after end of Chargeable Accounting Period
Income Tax	Tax year	31 January following tax year	31 January following tax year

1.3 **(a)** £37,700

(b) £3,188.70

1.4 **(a)**, **(b)**, **(c)** and **(d)** are true; **(e)** and **(f)** are false.

1.5 The final submission dates for tax returns are as follows:

A sole trader with accounts made up to 31 March 2024: **31 January 2025**

A limited company with accounts made up to 31 December 2023: **31 December 2024**

2 Corporation Tax – trading profits

2.1

	Add to net profit	Deduct from net profit	No adjustment required
Depreciation	✔		
Discount received			✔
Directors' salaries			✔
Dividends received		✔	
Rent receivable		✔	
Rent payable			✔
Interest payable			✔
Advertising costs			✔
Entertaining customers	✔		

2.2   The adjusted trading profit (before capital allowances) is:

(c)   £40,000   *Workings: (£37,000 – £12,000 + £13,000 + £2,000)*

2.3   **(a)**, **(d)** and **(g)** are true; **(b)**, **(c)**, **(e)** and **(f)** are false.

2.4   (e)   The trading profits for the long period are adjusted for tax purposes (before capital allowances), and the result is time-apportioned into two Chargeable Accounting Periods. Separate capital allowance computations are carried out for each Chargeable Accounting Period, and then deducted from each of the adjusted trading profits

2.5   The maximum amount of loss that could be set against the taxable total profits for 2022 is (a) £56,000 (the loss must first be set against the £25,000 investment income and gains of 2023 before it can be carried back to the previous year).

3   Corporation Tax – capital allowances

3.1

	Qualify	Do not qualify
Car for employee's private use	✔	
Office furniture	✔	
Capital expenditure on software	✔	
Payments for vehicle on operating lease		✔
Vehicles bought on credit	✔	
Buildings		✔
Equipment bought through hire purchase	✔	

3.2   The Full Expensing allowance that can be claimed is **£0**

The AIA that can be claimed is **£60,000**

The first year allowance that can be claimed at 100% is **£26,000**

The writing down allowance that can be claimed at 18% is **£0**

The writing down allowance that can be claimed at 6% is **£1,320**

The total capital allowance that can be claimed is **£87,320**

3.3

	AIA (to limit)	Main pool	Special rate pool	100% FYA	Full Expensing FYA
Car emissions of 185 g/km			✔		
Car emissions of 39 g/km		✔			
Machinery	✔				✔*
Zero-emission goods vehicle				✔	✔*
Car emissions of 105 g/km			✔		

* depending on date of purchase, and whether new or used.

3.4   **(b)** and **(d)** are true; **(a)**, **(c)** and **(e)** are false.

3.5   Capital Allowance Computation

	Full Expensing FYA £	Other FYA £	AIA £	Main Pool £	Special Rate Pool £	Capital Allowances £
WDV bf				120,000	19,000	
Acquisition Car (190 g/km)					35,000	
Acquisition New Machinery	60,000*					
Full Expensing	(60,000)*					60,000
Disposal Proceeds				(5,000)	(7,000)	
Sub Total				115,000	47,000	
18% WDA				(20,700)		20,700
6% WDA					(2,820)	2,820
WDV cf				94,300	44,180	
Total Capital Allowances						83,520

* AIA could alternatively be claimed

4 Corporation Tax – chargeable gains

4.1

	Actual proceeds	Market value	Zero
Sale of asset for £15,000 to Director who owns 80% of shares in company. Market value of asset is £35,000		✔	
Gift of asset to unconnected individual (non-shareholder)		✔	
Sale of asset to company employee (non- shareholder) at below market value	✔		
Destruction of an uninsured asset during fire			✔
Sale of asset for £15,000 to Director who owns 10% of shares in company. Market value of asset is £35,000	✔		
Shares owned in an unconnected company that have become worthless due to the company's liquidation			✔

4.2

	No. Shares	Cost £	Indexed Cost £
Purchase	8,000	19,500	19,500
Index to July 2003			2,223
Rights issue	200	360	360
Sub total	8,200	19,860	22,083
Index to December 2017			11,792
Sub total	8,200	19,860	33,875
Disposal	(6,000)	(14,532)	(24,787)
Pool balance	2,200	5,328	9,088

Proceeds	£30,000
Indexed Cost	£24,787
Gain	£5,213

4.3

	£	£
Proceeds		2,250,000
less		
Cost	560,000	
Extension	300,000	
		(860,000)
Unindexed gain		1,390,000
Indexation on cost	1,024,240	
Indexation on extension	315,300	
		1,339,540
Gain		50,460

4.4   (a)

	£	£
Proceeds		980,000
less		
Cost	500,000	
Indexation	364,500	
		864,500
Gain		115,500

All this gain will be chargeable, since it is less than the amount not reinvested (£980,000 – £850,000) = £130,000.

(b)   If a further amount is invested in another qualifying asset by September 2026, then some, or all, of the gain could be rolled over at that point.

5 Corporation Tax – calculating the tax

5.1

Loss	Rules that can apply
Trading Loss	(a) and (e)
Capital Loss	(f)
Rental Loss	(a)

5.2 **(a)**

Corporation Tax at main rate	£100,000 x 25%	£25,000
Less marginal relief 3/200 x (£166,667 - £100,000)		(£1,000)
		£24,000

(b)

FY 2022:	TTP £70,000 x main rate 19%	£13,300
FY 2023	TTP £210,000 x main rate* 25%	£52,500
		£65,800

*Limit in FY 2023 for 9 months is £187,500

(c)

Corporation Tax at main rate*	£65,000 x 25%	£16,250

*Limit is £250,000 / 4 = £62,500

5.3 **(b)**, **(c)**, **(e)**, **(f)** and **(g)** are true; **(a)** and **(d)** are false.

5.4

(a)	Minimum	0%	Maximum	30%
(b)	Minimum	50%	Maximum	100%
(c)	Minimum	30%	Maximum	100%

6   Income Tax – trading profits

6.1

	Badges of Trade
Reason for acquisition and sale of item(s)	✔
Whether individual enjoys carrying out the activity	
Whether there is a profit motive	✔
How long the individual has owned the item(s) before sale	✔
Whether the individual only sells via computer sites	
Whether any supplementary work is carried out on the item(s) before sale	✔
Whether the individual considers the activity to be his hobby	
How often the individual carries out similar transactions	✔
Whether the items bought and sold (the subject matter) are used personally by the individual before sale	✔

6.2

	Allowable expenditure	Non-allowable expenditure
Cost of sales	✔	
Entertaining staff	✔	
Fines for lawbreaking by business owner		✔
Gifts of food or drink to customers		✔
Trade bad debts written off	✔	
Salary and NIC of business owner		✔
Depreciation		✔
Loss on sale of non-current assets		✔

6.3

	£	£
Net Profit		112,310
Add		
Goods for own use	2,000	
Depreciation	22,020	
Laura's salary	45,000	
Laura's son's salary (unreasonable)	28,000	
Gifts of bottles of wine	2,400	
Laura's son's car expenses	3,800	
Increase in general bad debt provision	2,600	
	———	
		105,820
		———
		218,130
less		
Capital allowances		10,400
		———
Adjusted trading profits		207,730
		———

6.4   The AIA that can be claimed is **£44,400**[1]

The single asset pool writing down allowance that can be claimed is **£720**[2]

The main rate pool writing down allowance that can be claimed is **£0**

The total capital allowance that can be claimed is **£45,120**[3]

The total written down value carried forward is **£18,800**[4]

Workings:

(1)   £30,000 + (£18,000 × 80%) = £44,400 *(below AIA limit for this period.)*

(2)   £20,000 × 6% × 60% = £720

(3)   £44,400 + £720 = £45,120

(4)   £20,000 – (£20,000 × 6%) = £18,800

7 Income Tax – further issues

7.1 (b)   £37,000

The rules for a sole trader or partnership mean that the loss can be set off against the previous year's total income without first setting off in the current year.

7.2

	Total	Pete	Heather	Ash
	£	£	£	£
1 Jan – 31 August 2023	80,000	40,000	40,000	0
1 Sept – 31 Dec 2023	40,000	15,000	15,000	10,000
Total	120,000	55,000	55,000	10,000

7.3

		£
Payment on 31 January 2024	Balance of tax and NIC for 2022/23	3,600
	Payment on account for 2023/24	5,800
	Total	9,400
Payment on 31 July 2024	Payment on account for 2023/24	5,800

8 Business disposals and tax planning

8.1 **(a)**, **(d)**, **(f)** and **(g)** are true; **(b)**, **(c)** and **(e)** are false.

8.2 **(a)** They each meet the following criteria for Business Asset Disposal Relief:

- The shares are in a personal trading company
- They each own at least 5% of the ordinary shares (in their case 50%) which give them entitlement to voting rights, distributable profits and assets in a winding up
- They have owned the shares for more than two years
- They are both employees of the company

(b) The Capital Gains Tax for **each** individual will be calculated as:

	£
Disposal proceeds (15,000 shares at £18)	270,000
less Cost	(30,000)
Gain	240,000
less Annual Exempt Amount	(6,000)
Amount subject to CGT	234,000
CGT £234,000 x 10%	23,400

As they have not claimed Business Asset Disposal Relief previously, they have not yet used up the lifetime limit of £1,000,000 of gains.

8.3

	Salary	Dividends
Personal position:		
Income Tax rates range	20% - 40%	8.75% - 33.75%
Employees' NIC payable?	YES	NO
Company position:		
Corporation Tax % saving	19% - 26.5%	0%
Employers' NIC payable?	YES	NO

8.4 **Income Tax:**

Ellen would save Income Tax on her reduced salary at 40%, but she would pay 33.75% Income Tax on her dividends, after deducting the dividend allowance.

Brian would be able to utilise his personal allowance and dividend allowance against his dividends. He would pay a minimal amount of Income Tax at 8.75% on the remainder of his dividends.

Overall, the couple would pay less Income Tax than currently.

National Insurance:

The reduction in Ellen's salary would reduce her employees' contribution at 2%, and the company would reduce the employers' contribution of 13.8%.

There would be no NIC impact for Brian.

Corporation Tax:

The company currently pays Corporation Tax at 19% (the small profits rate) on the profits after deducting the salary and employers' NIC. If the salary were reduced then the taxable profits would increase by the reduction in salary plus employers' NIC, and this would be subject to Corporation Tax at 19%, or the main rate 25% less marginal relief if profits exceed £50,000 pa. The dividend payments would not affect Corporation Tax.

Practice
assessment 1

Task 1

(a)   From the following list, select the correct treatment of each item when computing taxable trading profits, by ticking the appropriate column.

		Disallow and add back	Disallow and deduct	Allow (no action)
(a)	Discount received			
(b)	Loss on sale of non-current asset			
(c)	Gifts of chocolates (with logo) costing £20 each to customers			
(d)	Rental income			
(e)	Installation of new production machinery			
(f)	Advertising expenditure			

(b)   Identify whether the following statements are true or false.

Statement	True	False
Dividend income is not part of taxable trading income, either for limited companies or for unincorporated businesses		
Salaries of directors are allowable costs for limited companies, but owners' salaries are not allowable costs for unincorporated businesses		

Task 2

(a)   A company has the following information regarding its non-current assets for a 12-month CAP, ending on 31/3/2024.

	£
Written down values brought forward:	
General (main) pool	105,000
Special rate pool	17,000
Additions:	
Computer System (new)	890,000
New car for Sales Director (zero emissions)	25,000
Disposals:	
Machinery	5,000

Calculate the maximum capital allowances for the CAP, using the following table:

	Full Expensing FYA £	Other FYA £	AIA £	Main Pool £	Special Rate Pool £	Capital Allowances £
WDV bf						

(b) Delta Limited purchased a warehouse from Alpha Limited for £800,000 on 1 August 2023, and immediately started using it in its trade. The price included land valued at £200,000.

Alpha Ltd was the building's first owner, and it had been claiming structures and buildings allowance (SBA) at a rate of £15,000 per year from 2019 until the sale.

Delta Limited has a year-end of 31 March.

Explain and calculate the qualifying cost and the claim that Delta Limited can make for SBA for the CAP year ended 31 March 2024.

Task 3

Molly and Nigel are in partnership, trading as carpet fitters, with an accounting year-end of 31 March. They had shared profits 3:2 for some time. On 1 November 2023 their arrangements changed to the rates shown below.

	Molly	**Nigel**
Salary per year	£12,000	£18,000
Partners' capital	£48,000	£18,000
Interest on capital	4% pa	4% pa
Profit sharing percentage	55%	45%

The taxable profit of the partnership for the year ended 31 March 2024 was £109,920.

(a) Show the division of the profits between the partners for the year ended 31 March 2024 using the table below. Round answers to the nearest £ if appropriate.

To 31 October 2023	Molly £	Nigel £
Share of profits		
From 1 November 2023	**Molly £**	**Nigel £**
Interest on capital		
Salary		
Share of profits		

(b) Calculate Molly's National Insurance Contributions for 2023/24. Round answers to the nearest penny.

	£
Class 2 NIC	
Class 4 NIC at 9%	
Class 4 NIC at 2%	

Task 4

(a)   Gamma plc sold a shop for £980,000 on 1 August 2023 that it had acquired for £230,000 on 1 January 1993. Gamma had extended the shop at a cost of £80,000 on 1 June 2002.

In December 2024 Gamma purchased a warehouse for £850,000.

Indexation factors are as follows:

January 1993 – December 2017   1.017

June 2002 – December 2017   0.578

Complete the following table to calculate the chargeable gains on the sale of the shop, assuming any reliefs are claimed.

	£
Proceeds	
Original cost	
Enhancement expenditure	
Indexation on original cost	
Indexation on enhancement expenditure	
Total gain	
Gain chargeable immediately	
Gain deferred	

(b)   Select the appropriate statement.

If a company has claimed structures and buildings allowance on a building that it then sells at a gain, the effect will be:

The chargeable gain will be reduced by the total SBA already claimed	
The SBA will have no effect on the chargeable gain	
The chargeable gain will be increased by the total SBA already claimed	

Task 5

Perfect Ltd bought 9,000 shares in Toronto Ltd for £27,900 in October 2001. Bonus shares were issued in April 2002 at 1 for 10. Purchases of 5,000 shares were made in July 2003 for £3.80 per share. In April 2023, Perfect Ltd sold 10,000 of the shares for £6.00 per share.

Indexation factors were:

October 2001 to July 2003: 0.114

July 2003 to December 2017: 0.534

Calculate the pool balances remaining and the gain made on the share disposal.

	No. Shares	Cost £	Indexed Cost £
October 2001 purchase	9,000	27,900	27,900
April 2002 bonus 1:10	900		
	9,900	27,900	27,900
Indexation Oct 01 – July 03			3,180.60
			31,080.60
July 2003 purchase	5,000	19,000	19,000
	14,900	46,900	50,080.60
Indexation July 03 – Dec 17			26,743.04
	14,900	46,900	76,823.64
April 2023 disposal	(10,000)	(31,476.51)	(51,559.49)
Pool balance c/f	4,900	15,423.49	25,264.15

Proceeds	£ 60,000.00
Indexed Cost	£ 51,559.49
Gain	£ 8,440.51

Task 6

(a) Delta Limited has produced the following results for the 16-month accounting period to 31 December 2023.

Trading Profits for 16-month period (before capital allowances)		£800,000
Capital Allowances:	12 months to 31/8/2023	£54,000
	4 months to 31/12/2023	£19,000
Chargeable Gains:	Disposal 12/12/2022	£36,000
	Disposal 19/4/2023	£14,000
	Disposal 10/10/2023	£41,000
Rental Income – monthly amount		£2,000
Qualifying Charitable Donation (paid 31/12/2023)		£6,000

Use the following table to calculate the TTP for each CAP.

	CAP 12 months to 31/8/2023 £	CAP 4 months to 31/12/2023 £
Trading Profits before CAs		
Capital Allowances		
Trading Profits		
Chargeable Gains		
Rental Income		
Sub total		
QCD		
TTP		

(b) Calculate the Corporation Tax payable by Delta Limited for the two accounting periods.

	CAP 12 months to 31/8/2023 £	CAP 4 months to 31/12/2023 £
Corporation Tax Payable		

Task 7

(a) Sue has been trading for many years, and her Income Tax and NIC Class 4 liability is as follows:

2020/21	£15,600
2021/22	£18,100
2022/23	£19,300

Complete the following table to show the details and amounts that Sue will pay in the calendar year 2024.

Tax year (YYYY/YY)	Payment date (DD/MM/YYYY)	Payment on account / Balancing payment	Amount £

(b) National Limited has an accounting year-end of 31 August 2023. The final date for payment of Corporation Tax for this CAP is:

(c) Identify whether each of the following statements is true or false.

		True	False
(a)	Interest is payable by self-employed individuals on late balancing payments and underpayments of amounts due on account		
(b)	A £100 late submission penalty is payable for self-employed individuals only if their tax return is late by more than 60 days		
(c)	A 'reasonable excuse' by an individual for a late return may be sufficient to prevent a penalty if HMRC considers it to be valid		
(d)	If a taxpayer took reasonable care, yet the return still contained an error, there will be no penalty		
(e)	A sole trader who starts trading must notify HMRC within six months of the end of tax year		
(f)	If HMRC completes an enquiry into a company and submits a closure notice, the company has 30 days to appeal the decision		

(d) Marmalade Limited made an unprompted disclosure of an error which was considered to be due to lack of reasonable care. The additional Corporation Tax payable as a result was £1,500. The penalty will be as follows:

Minimum £	
Maximum £	

Task 8

It is May 2024. A new client, David, has come to you to ask for advice. David is a Director and sole shareholder of a limited company that started trading on 1 January 2022. HMRC were notified that trading had started, but no other contact has been made with HMRC regarding Corporation Tax.

Accounts have been prepared for the year ended 31 December 2022 and it has been calculated that the Corporation Tax for that period will be £19,000. Unfortunately, since the accounts were prepared, many of the sales and purchase invoices for the period were accidentally shredded.

(a) Write a note that explains what deadlines have been missed and what penalties and/or interest the company could be liable for based on the above information.

(b) David currently pays himself a salary of £60,000, and he has no other income. He is considering whether he could also pay dividends to both himself and his wife, and how this could be arranged, and what the tax implications would be. David's wife is an additional rate taxpayer.

Write notes that would respond to David's enquiry.

Task 9

Jack joined Jonah in partnership on 1 April 2022, sharing profits equally. The results for the partnership were as follows:

Year ended 31 March 2023 £20,000 profit

Year ended 31 March 2024 £50,000 loss

Year ended 31 March 2025 £60,000 profit (estimated)

Jack has regular property income of £15,000 per year. Apart from this, he had no other income in the three years before the partnership started, since he was a student.

Jonah was employed, earning £50,000 per year for each of the three years before the partnership started. He has no other income.

(a)   Explain the options for Jack for setting off his share of the partnership loss. Recommend which option would be most tax efficient.

(b) Explain the options for Jonah for setting off his share of the partnership loss. Recommend which option would be most tax efficient.

Task 10

Sonia had operated as a sole trader for many years. She decided to sell her business as a going concern in August 2023.

The overall proceeds were £950,000, and these were agreed with the purchaser as relating to the following assets.

	Proceeds £
Goodwill	150,000
Buildings	500,000
Plant and machinery	100,000
Van	30,000
Net current assets	170,000

Some goodwill had been acquired by Sonia in 2010, when she bought the intangible assets of another business for £20,000. The buildings cost Sonia £350,000 in 2007. The plant and machinery and van have a tax written down value of £35,000 in the main pool.

Sonia had previously claimed Entrepreneur's Relief (the forerunner of Business Asset Disposal Relief) on gains of £800,000. Sonia is a higher rate taxpayer. She had no other disposals in the tax year 2023/24.

(a) Complete the following table to calculate the Capital Gains Tax on the business disposal. Use zeros if appropriate.

	Capital Gain £
Goodwill	
Buildings	
Plant and machinery	
Van	
Net current assets	
Total gains	
Annual Exempt Amount	
Gain charged at 10%	
Gain charged at 20%	

(b) Select the statements that are true regarding Sonia's disposal of her business.

	True
The disposal will result in a balancing charge in the main pool for capital allowances	
The impact of the disposal on the capital allowances will result in a reduction in trading profits	
Sonia can make no further claims for Business Asset Disposal Relief in the future	

Practice assessment 2

Task 1

Lisa has the following income statement:

		£
Gross profit		1,450,395
Wages and salaries	731,200	
Accountancy and legal costs	21,450	
Motor expenses	65,480	
Repairs and renewals	55,550	
Office expenses	42,690	
Depreciation	155,310	
Other expenses	41,840	1,113,520
Profit		336,875

Notes include:

Gross profit is after deducting bulk discounts given of   £15,300

Wages and salaries include:

Lisa's salary and personal pension contributions   £75,400

Lisa's son's salary (he works part-time in the office)   £7,400

Accountancy and legal costs comprise:

Legal fees to purchase new office building   £10,250

Annual accountancy and audit fee   £11,200

Motor expenses include:

Operating lease of 180 g/km car used for business by works manager   £11,660

Expenses of Lisa's car which is used 70% for the business   £12,500

Repairs and renewals include:

Repainting exterior of factory building   £40,000

Capital allowances have been calculated as   £21,380

(a) Complete the following computation. You may not need to use all the lines provided.

	£
Profit	336,875
Disallowed items added back:	
Allowed items deducted:	
Adjusted trading profits	

(b) Complete the following table by selecting the correct treatment of each item in the accounts of a sole trader when adjusting for tax purposes.

	Add back to profit	Deduct from profit	No adjustment required
(a) Loss on sale of non-current assets			
(b) Installation costs of new machinery			
(c) Discounts received for prompt payment			
(d) Interest received on deposit account			

Task 2

Tintagel Limited had the following non-current asset information for the seven month period ending on 31 March 2024.

Balances brought forward on 1 September 2023:

General pool	£157,500
Special rate pool	£31,680

Additions during period:

Machinery (used)	£606,000
Car (CO_2 emissions 0 g/km)	£29,500

The company was forced to cease trading on 30 June 2024, following an irrecoverable debt from a major customer.

The proceeds of the non-current assets that were sold on that date were:

Car purchased in previous CAP	£19,800
General pool machinery (including where AIA claimed)	£255,500
Special rate pool items	£22,100

Calculate the capital allowances for the CAP ended 31 March 2024, and the final CAP ended 30 June 2024. Use the table on the next page.

	Full Expensing FYA £	Other FYA £	AIA £	Main Pool £	Special Rate Pool £	Capital Allowances £

Task 3

(a) Olly and Pete are in partnership, working as plasterers, with an accounting year-end of 31 March. They had shared profits equally for some time. On 1 September 2023 their arrangements changed as shown below.

	Olly	**Pete**
Salary per year	£15,000	£12,000
Partners' capital	£30,000	£24,000
Interest on capital	5% pa	5% pa
Profit sharing percentage	40%	60%

The taxable profit of the partnership for the year ended 31 March 2024 was £92,160.

Show the division of the profits between the partners for the year ended 31 March 2024 using the table below. Round answers to the nearest £ if appropriate.

To 31 August 2023	**Olly £**	**Pete £**
Share of profits		
From 1 September 2023	**Olly £**	**Pete £**
Interest on capital		
Salary		
Share of profits		

(b) The partnership agreement of Brian and Colin stipulates that Brian is entitled to 55% of partnership profits and Colin 45%.

The total partnership profits for 2023/24 were £99,600.

Complete the following table and calculate the Class 4 National Insurance Contributions for both Brian and Colin for 2023/24. Calculations should be carried out to the nearest penny.

	Profits £	**Class 4 at 9%** £	**Class 4 at 2%** £	**Total Class 4 NIC** £
Brian				
Colin				

Task 4

(a)   Dickinson Limited sold an asset in April 2023 for £43,500. The costs of disposal were £300. The asset was bought in August 2000 for £19,850 plus buying costs of £650.

The indexation factor from August 2000 to December 2017 is 0.631.

Calculate the chargeable gain on the disposal of this asset using the following table. Enter zero against any costs that are not allowable.

	£	£
Proceeds		
Disposal costs		
Cost		
Buying costs		
Indexation allowance		
Gain		

(b)   Exe Limited plans to sell some land on 15 January 2024. It estimates that the proceeds will be £1,540,000, and the gain resulting from the sale will be £453,000.

If Exe Limited wishes to defer the gain by using rollover relief, the earliest date that qualifying asset(s) can be acquired is [   ]

and the latest is [   ].

To obtain deferment of the whole gain, the qualifying asset(s) must cost at least

£ [   ].

Task 5

Gamma plc has had various transactions of shares in Wye Limited, as follows:

Date	Transaction
1 January 1992	Purchased 5,000 shares for £22,500
1 January 1995	Received bonus shares of 1 for 4
1 December 2001	Purchased shares through 1 for 2 rights issue at £6.50 each
15 April 2023	Purchased 1,500 shares at £12.00 each
20 April 2023	Sold 5,000 shares for £65,000

The following indexation factors are available:

January 1992 to January 1995	0.077
January 1995 to December 2001	0.188
January 1992 to December 2001	0.279
December 2001 to December 2017	0.604

(a)   Complete the following share pool for Gamma plc, including the balance of shares carried forward. Round to nearest £ where necessary.

Date & Details	Number	Cost £	Indexed Cost £

(b) Calculate the chargeable gain or allowable loss on the disposal of shares in Wye Limited by Gamma plc in the year ended 31 December 2023.

Task 6

(a)   Team Limited made up accounts for the 17 month period to 31 August 2023. The following details have been extracted for the period.

The company made a capital loss of £14,150 in February 2023, and capital gains of £19,660 in December 2022 and £19,475 in May 2023. The adjusted trading profits for the period were £160,871.

State the amounts to be taken into account in each of the following periods.

	First accounting period £	**Second accounting period** £
Capital gains		
Trading profits		
TTP		

(b)   Calculate the Corporation Tax payable by Team Limited for the two accounting periods.

	First accounting period £	**Second accounting period** £
Corporation Tax at main rate		
Less marginal relief		
Corporation Tax payable		

Task 7

(a) Adam has been trading for many years, and his Income Tax and Class 4 NIC liability is as follows:

2020/21   £9,600

2021/22   £15,450

2022/23   £13,500

Adam has not made any claim to reduce payments on account.

Complete the following table to show the total amounts that Adam will pay on the dates shown.

Payment date	Amount £
31 July 2023	
31 January 2024	
31 July 2024	

(b) Chef Limited has an accounting year-end of 31 July 2023. The final date for payment of Corporation Tax for this CAP is:

(c) Identify whether each of the following statements is true or false.

		True	False
(a)	Interest is payable by self-employed individuals on late balancing payments, but not on underpayments of amounts due on account		
(b)	A total late submission penalty is payable for self-employed individuals of £100, plus £10 per day, if their tax return is late by between three and six months		
(c)	Online and paper-based returns have the same submission deadlines for individuals		
(d)	If a taxpayer took reasonable care, yet the return still contained an error, there can be a penalty		
(e)	A sole trader who fails to keep adequate records for the correct length of time can face a penalty of £3,000 per tax year		
(f)	Companies must submit a tax return online for each Chargeable Accounting Period		

(d) Carrington Limited made a prompted disclosure of an error which was considered to be due to lack of reasonable care. The additional Corporation Tax payable as a result was £4,500. The penalty will be as follows:

Minimum £
Maximum £

Task 8

Jonathan is a sole trader, who has an annual profit of about £70,000, and takes drawings of £3,000 per month. Jonathan's wife Sue helps in the business by taking orders and dealing with paperwork and accounts. Sue's only income is interest from a savings account of £1,000 per year. Jonathan is considering employing Sue in the business at a salary of £15,000, but he is worried that this may be considered as tax evasion.

(a) Differentiate between tax evasion and tax planning, and also explain which of these Jonathan would be carrying out by employing Sue.

(b) Explain how Jonathan and his business are currently subject to Income Tax and National Insurance Contributions.

(c) Explain the impact on Income Tax and NIC for Jonathan and Sue of employing Sue in the business, and also note any practical issues.

Suggest an alternative way that Sue could be formally involved in the business.

Task 9

(a)   Tulip Limited has the following results from the last two years.

Year ended	31 March 2024	31 March 2023
	£	£
Trading profit (loss)	(41,250)	10,680
Chargeable gain (loss)	(5,650)	15,400
Rental profit	12,000	12,000
Qualifying Charitable Donation	1,800	1,800

Tulip Limited has a policy of always claiming relief for losses as soon as possible.

Complete the following table to show how Tulip Limited would claim for its losses.

	£
How much trading loss can be claimed against income in the year ended 31 March 2024?	
How much trading loss can be claimed against income in the year ended 31 March 2023?	
How much trading loss can be carried forward to the year ended 31 March 2025?	
How much capital loss can be carried forward against capital gains in the year ended 31 March 2025?	
How much QCD can be set against income in the year ended 31 March 2023?	
How much QCD can be set against income in the year ended 31 March 2024?	
How much QCD can be carried forward to be set against income in the year ended 31 March 2025?	

(b)   Chantelle has run her sole trader business successfully for many years, until the business ceased when it became unviable following a large trading loss. The loss of £45,000 was incurred in the final twelve months trading and related to 2023/24.

Chantelle's trading and other income for the last few tax years was as follows:

	2020/21	**2021/22**	**2022/23**	**2023/24**
Trading Income £	20,000	26,500	21,000	0
Other Income £	12,500	12,500	12,500	12,500

Explain what Chantelle's options are for offsetting her loss. Recommend, with reasons, which option should be followed.

Task 10

Mark had operated as a sole trader for many years since his uncle originally gave him a shop, and they jointly claimed gift relief. He decided to sell his business as a going concern in December 2023.

The overall proceeds were £630,000, and these were agreed with the purchaser as relating to the following assets.

	Proceeds £
Goodwill	50,000
Shop building	500,000
Shop fittings	20,000
Inventory	60,000

The shop had a market value of £280,000 when it was given to Mark, and the gift relief at that time totalled £110,000.

Plant and machinery capital allowances have been claimed on the shop fittings since they were acquired for £85,000. There is no balance in the main pool for capital allowances. The inventory valuation in the sale is based on cost.

Mark has not previously claimed Entrepreneur's Relief or Business Asset Disposal Relief. Mark is a higher rate taxpayer. He had no other disposals in the tax year 2023/24.

(a)   Complete the following table to calculate the Capital Gains Tax on the business disposal. Use zeros if appropriate.

	Capital Gain £
Goodwill	
Shop building	
Shop fittings	
Inventory	
Total gains	
Annual Exempt Amount	
Taxable Amount	
Capital Gains Tax	

(b)   Select any statements that are true regarding Mark's disposal of his business.

	True
The disposal will result in a balancing allowance in the main pool for capital allowances	
The impact of the disposal on the capital allowances will result in a reduction in trading profits	
The sale of inventory at cost will not increase Mark's taxable profits	

Practice assessment 3

Task 1

(a)   Analyse the tax treatment of the following items in a sole trader's trading income computation by ticking the appropriate column.

	Add back to net profit	Deduct from net profit	No adjustment required
(a) Bank interest receivable			
(b) Bank interest payable			
(c) Increase in general provision for irrecoverable debts			
(d) Profit on sale of non-current assets			
(e) Staff travelling expenses			
(f) Owner's class 2 & 4 NIC			
(g) Discounts receivable			

(b)   Lemming Limited has the following statement of profit or loss:

	£	£
Gross profit		1,980,560
Wages and salaries	863,200	
Accountancy and legal costs	48,450	
Motor expenses	121,680	
Repairs and renewals	130,500	
Office expenses	82,600	
Depreciation	245,110	
Other expenses	88,840	1,580,380
Profit		400,180

Notes include:

Wages and salaries include:

Directors' salaries and personal pension contributions	£175,000

Accountancy and legal costs include:

Legal fees to renew 10 year lease on office building	£4,120
Taxation advice	£3,550
Annual accountancy and audit fee	£11,200

Motor expenses include:

Operating lease of 180 g/km car used for business by Director (50% private use)	£9,860

Repairs and renewals include:

Replacement of office furniture	£12,000

Capital allowances have been calculated as	£33,780

Complete the following computation. You may not need to use all the lines provided.

	£
Profit	400,180
Disallowed items added back:	
Allowed items deducted:	
Adjusted trading profits	

Task 2

(a) A company has the following information regarding its non-current assets for an 8-month CAP ending on 31/12/2023.

	£
Written down values brought forward:	
General (main) pool	125,000
Special rate pool	47,000
Additions:	
Computer System (new)	905,000
New car for Sales Director (emissions 170 g/km)	28,000
Disposals:	
Machinery	5,000

Calculate the total capital allowances and show the balances to carry forward to the next accounting period, using the following table.

	Full Expensing FYA £	Other FYA £	AIA £	Main Pool £	Special Rate Pool £	Capital Allowances £

(b)   Wessex Limited had a new factory built, which it brought into use on 1 December 2023.

(i)   From the following list of costs and dates incurred, select those that will be eligible costs for structures and buildings allowance.

Date	Cost	Amount £	Eligible for SBA
1 April 2022	Purchase of land	560,000	
25 May 2022	Planning permission fees	4,500	
31 August 2022	Factory design fees	65,000	
30 September 2022	Site preparation work	155,000	
30 January 2023	Construction interim payment	475,000	
1 November 2023	Construction final payment	325,000	
31 January 2024	Purchase of fixed machinery	175,000	

(ii)   State the date from which SBA will be claimable

Task 3

(a) Adam, Ben and Clive have been in partnership for many years, sharing profits in the ratio 5:3:2. They have always made their accounts up to 31 March each year. On 31 August 2023, Clive left the partnership. On 1 September 2023 Catherine joined the partnership. From that point onwards, Adam and Ben received salaries of £24,000 per year, and Catherine received a salary of £6,000 per year. The remaining profits were divided equally.

For the year ended 31 March 2024 the partnership trading profit was £360,000.

Complete the following table to show the division of profits for the year ended 31 March 2024.

	Total £	Adam £	Ben £	Clive £	Catherine £
Period to 31 August					
Period from 1 September					
Salaries					
Share Balance					
Total for year					

(b) Calculate Ben's National Insurance Contributions for 2023/24. Round answers to the nearest penny.

	£
Class 2 NIC	
Class 4 NIC at 9%	
Class 4 NIC at 2%	

Task 4

Zed plc sold a factory for £1,790,000 on 1 December 2023 that it had acquired for £830,000 on 1 June 2002. Zed plc had extended the factory at a cost of £425,000 on 1 January 2019.

In November 2024 Zed plc purchased a warehouse for £1,850,000.

Indexation factors are as follows:

June 2002 – December 2017   0.578

Complete the following table to calculate the chargeable gains on the sale of the factory, assuming any reliefs are claimed.

	£
Proceeds	
Original cost	
Enhancement expenditure	
Indexation on original cost	
Indexation on enhancement expenditure	
Total gain	
Gain chargeable immediately	
Gain deferred	
Base cost of warehouse	

Task 5

Bee Ltd bought 5,000 shares in Wye Ltd for £15,900 in October 2001. Bonus shares were issued in April 2002 at 1 for 10. A purchase of 2,000 shares was made on 20 April 2023 for £4.80 per share. On 25 April 2023 Bee Ltd sold 3,000 of the shares for £4.95 per share.

Indexation factors were:

October 2001 to December 2017: 0.596

Clearly showing the matching of the shares, calculate the gain or loss on the sale of shares and any pool balances remaining.

Task 6

(a) Florinda Limited has produced the following results for the 17-month accounting period to 31 December 2023.

Trading Profits for 17-month period (before capital allowances)		£714,000
Capital Allowances:	12 months to 31/7/2023	£74,000
	5 months to 31/12/2023	£41,000
Chargeable Gains:	Disposal 12/12/2022	£33,000
	Disposal 19/6/2023	(£44,000) loss
	Disposal 10/11/2023	£17,000
Rental Income – monthly amount		£3,100
Qualifying Charitable Donation (paid 31/12/2023)		£6,000

Use the following table to calculate the TTP for each CAP.

	CAP 12 months to 31/7/2023 £	CAP 5 months to 31/12/2023 £
Trading Profits before CAs		
Capital Allowances		
Trading Profits		
Chargeable Gains		
Rental Income		
Sub total		
QCD		
TTP		

(b) Calculate the Corporation Tax Liability (to the nearest £) for each of the following unconnected companies.

(i) Company A has a 9 month CAP ending on 31/12/2023 with TTP of £120,000. It has no associated companies.

```
┌─────────────────────────────┐
│                             │
│                             │
│                             │
└─────────────────────────────┘
```

(ii) Company B has a 12 month CAP ending on 31/12/2023 with TTP of £360,000. It has no associated companies.

```
┌─────────────────────────────┐
│                             │
│                             │
│                             │
└─────────────────────────────┘
```

(iii) Company C has a 12 month CAP ending on 31/3/2024 with TTP of £95,000. It has one associated company.

```
┌─────────────────────────────┐
│                             │
│                             │
│                             │
└─────────────────────────────┘
```

Task 7

(a)   Alison has been trading for many years, and her Income Tax and Class 4 NIC liability is as follows:

2020/21   £19,250

2021/22   £18,400

2022/23   £21,500

Alison has not made any claim to reduce payments on account.

Complete the following table to show the total amounts that Alison will pay on the dates shown.

Payment date	Amount £
31 July 2023	
31 January 2024	
31 July 2024	

(b)   Cannie Limited has an accounting year-end of 31 May 2023. The final date for submission of the CT600 tax return is:

(c)   Identify whether each of the following statements is true or false.

		True	False
(a)	Interest is payable by self-employed individuals on underpayments of amounts due on account, but not on balancing payments		
(b)	A total late submission penalty is payable for self-employed individuals of £1,000 for tax returns late by six months		
(c)	Online returns have later submission deadlines than paper-based returns for individuals		
(d)	A late payment of the balancing payment of Income Tax of between 30 days and six months will incur a penalty of 5% of the tax due		
(e)	A tax advisor is liable for a penalty if they assist in making an incorrect return		
(f)	Companies must notify HMRC within three months of starting to trade		

(d) Guy Collins Limited made a prompted disclosure of an error which was considered deliberate, but not concealed. The additional Corporation Tax payable as a result was £40,500. The penalty will be as follows:

Minimum £	
Maximum £	

Task 8

(a) You work for a small firm of accountants. One of your clients is a self-employed car dealer, and an additional rate taxpayer. He has arrived for a meeting that he requested.

He explains that he has been introduced by a friend at his golf club to a tax consultant who has recommended that he joins a tax avoidance scheme. The tax advisor has told him that this will reduce his normal tax liability by a substantial amount, and that it must be legal since HMRC is aware of the scheme.

The client is keen to go ahead, and asks you to explain the differences between tax avoidance and tax evasion, and any implications of joining the scheme. He also requests details of other clients that have considered or joined such schemes.

Give your response in the box below, under the headings given. Include consideration of the ethical implications for you and your practice.

Tax avoidance and tax evasion

Implications of joining the scheme

Details of other clients

Ethical implications for you and your practice

(b) Julian has started a limited company as the sole shareholder. He has other income consisting of dividends from an investment of £3,000 per year. Since the company has negotiated a long-term contract, he is able to predict the company profits accurately at £75,000 per year (before extraction of salary or dividends).

Julian currently takes a salary of £47,270 from the company, which is all taxed at basic rate Income Tax. Employers' NIC has been calculated at £5,267 per year.

(i) Explain how much Corporation Tax will currently be payable, and how much profit will remain in the company that could be taken as dividends.

(ii) Explain how Corporation Tax, Income Tax, and NIC would be affected if Julian took the maximum dividends in addition to his salary.

Task 9

(a)   A limited company has the following tax-adjusted results for the 12-month CAPs ending on 31 March:

	2022	2023	2024
	£	£	£
Trading profits	120,500	0	375,000
Trading loss		85,000	
Chargeable gain	50,300		
Capital loss		20,100	
Rental income	10,800	12,400	14,200

(i)   Assuming that the company wishes to claim any loss relief as early as possible, complete the following table. Insert zeros into any cells that do not apply.

	2022	2023	2024
	£	£	£
Trading profits			
Net chargeable gains			
Rental income			
Trading loss offset against taxable total profits			
Taxable total profits after offsetting losses			

(ii)   State briefly one disadvantage of the above method of trading loss relief, compared with carrying the loss forward to set against TTP of year ended 31 March 2024.

(b) George has run his unincorporated business for many years. He incurred a loss of £32,000 in 2022/23, but the business recovered the following year, and is continuing.

The following is a summary of George's income from his business and elsewhere for the last few years.

Tax Year	2020/21	2021/22	2022/23	2023/24
Trading Income £	25,000	28,000	0	18,000
Other Income £	10,000	14,000	13,000	12,000

George is concerned about cash flow, and would prefer an early tax reduction, provided it does not reduce the overall benefit of offsetting the loss by too much.

Outline briefly the options that George has for offsetting his loss. Recommend and explain the best solution, based on George's requirements.

Task 10

Emily had operated as a sole trader for many years. She decided to sell her business as a going concern in April 2023. Her profits before capital allowances for the final period are £40,000.

The overall proceeds were £300,000, and these were agreed with the purchaser as relating to the following assets.

	Proceeds £
Goodwill	50,000
Machinery	85,000
Car	20,000
Net current assets	145,000

Plant and machinery main pool has a tax written down value of £35,000. The machinery was originally purchased for £180,000. There are no other capital allowance pools. The car is a zero-emission model which had 100% FYA claimed on its cost of £45,000 in 2021.

(a) Complete the following table to calculate the capital gains on the business disposal. Use zeros if appropriate.

	Capital Gain £
Goodwill	
Machinery	
Car	
Net current assets	
Total gains	

(b) Calculate the total plant and machinery balancing charge that will arise from the disposal of the business.

Total balancing charge	£

(c) Select any of the following statements that are true.

	True
The calculation of the balancing charge in the main pool for capital allowances will incorporate the disposal proceeds of the car	
The reduction in profits due to the balancing charge could result in a terminal loss	

Answers to practice assessment 1

Task 1

(a) **(a)** and **(f)** Allow (no action); **(b)**, **(c)** and **(e)** Disallow and add back; **(d)** Disallow and deduct

(b)

Statement	True	False
Dividend income is not part of taxable trading income, either for limited companies or for unincorporated businesses	✔	
Salaries of directors are allowable costs for limited companies, but owners' salaries are not allowable costs for unincorporated businesses	✔	

Task 2 (a)

	Full Expensing FYA £	Other FYA £	AIA £	Main Pool £	Special Rate Pool £	Capital Allowances £
WDV bf				105,000	17,000	
Acquisition Car 0 g/km		25,000				
100% FYA		(25,000)				25,000
Acquisition Computer	890,000*					
Full Expensing	(890,000)*					890,000
Disposal Proceeds				(5,000)		
Sub Totals				100,000	17,000	
18% WDA				(18,000)		18,000
6% WDA					(1,020)	1,020
WDV cf				82,000	15,980	
Capital Allowances						934,020

* AIA could alternatively be claimed

(b)

> Delta Limited's claim will be based on the qualifying cost that the original owner had spent on the warehouse. Since Alpha Limited was claiming £15,000 per year, the qualifying cost would be £15,000 / 3% = £500,000. This would not have included land.
>
> Delta Limited's claim for the year ended 31 March 2024 will be based on the time that it used the warehouse for a qualifying purpose.
>
> This will be 8/12 x £500,000 x 3% = £10,000.

Task 3

(a)

To 31 October 2023	Molly £	Nigel £
Share of profits	38,472	25,648
From 1 November 2023	**Molly £**	**Nigel £**
Interest on capital	800	300
Salary	5,000	7,500
Share of profits	17,710	14,490

(b)

	£
Class 2 NIC	179.40
Class 4 NIC at 9%	3,393.00
Class 4 NIC at 2%	234.24

Task 4

(a)

	£
Proceeds	980,000
Original cost	230,000
Enhancement expenditure	80,000
Indexation on original cost	233,910
Indexation on enhancement expenditure	46,240
Total gain	389,850
Gain chargeable immediately	130,000
Gain deferred	259,850

(b)   The chargeable gain will be increased by the total SBA already claimed

Task 5

	No. Shares	Cost £	Indexed Cost £
Purchase October 2001	9,000	27,900	27,900
Bonus shares	900	0	0
Indexation to July 2003			3,181
Purchase July 2003	5,000	19,000	19,000
Sub total	14,900	46,900	50,081
Indexation to Dec 2017			26,743
Total	14,900	46,900	76,824
Disposal	(10,000)	(31,477)	(51,560)
Pool Balance	4,900	15,423	25,264

Proceeds	£60,000
Indexed Cost	£51,560
Gain	£8,440

Task 6

(a)

	CAP 12 months to 31/8/2023 £	CAP 4 months to 31/12/2023 £
Trading Profits before CAs	600,000	200,000
Capital Allowances	54,000	19,000
Trading Profits	546,000	181,000
Chargeable Gains	50,000	41,000
Rental Income	24,000	8,000
Sub total	620,000	230,000
QCD	0	6,000
TTP	620,000	224,000

(b)

	CAP 12 months to 31/8/2023 £	CAP 4 months to 31/12/2023 £
Corporation Tax Payable	133,300*	56,000

* (7/12 at 19%) + (5/12 at 25%)

Task 7

(a)

Tax year (YYYY/YY)	Payment date (DD/MM/YYYY)	Payment on account / Balancing payment	Amount £
2022/23	31/01/2024	Balancing payment	1,200
2023/24	31/01/2024	Payment on account	9,650
2023/24	31/07/2024	Payment on account	9,650

(b)   1 June 2024

(c)   **(b)** is False; the remaining statements are True

(d)

Minimum £	0
Maximum £	450

Task 8

(a)

> The Corporation Tax Return (CT600) for the year ended 31 December 2022 should have been filed by 31 December 2023. The penalty for submitting over three months late is £200. If the return is now submitted promptly it should avoid a further penalty which could be imposed of 10% of the Corporation Tax (ie £1,900) for submissions over six months late.
>
> The final payment of Corporation Tax for the year ended 31 December 2022 should have been made by 1 October 2023. Interest will be payable from that date until payment is made. The company is not liable to make instalment payments.
>
> There is a penalty for failing to keep appropriate records. This is up to £3,000 per Chargeable Accounting Period. Provided the missing records only relate to 2022 then only one penalty of £3,000 may be charged.
>
> Looking forward, the tax return for the year ended 31 December 2023 should be filed by 31 December 2024, with the tax payment made by 1 October 2024.

(b)

> Since David is currently the sole shareholder of the company, he would need to transfer some shares to his wife to enable her to receive dividends. This would have no implications for Capital Gains Tax.
>
> Dividends that were paid from the company profits are not tax-deductible for Corporation Tax purposes, so would not alter the taxable profits (currently £100,000) in the future.
>
> After deducting the dividend allowance, David would pay Income Tax at 33.75% on dividends that he received, while David's wife would pay 39.35%. This is because David is a higher rate taxpayer, while his wife is an additional rate taxpayer. The couple may wish to consider this when deciding to transfer any shares.
>
> Dividends are not subject to employees' or employers' NIC.

Task 9

(a)

> Under the general loss provisions, Jack could set his £25,000 share of the loss against his property income of £15,000 for 2023/24 and/or against his total income of £25,000 for 2022/23. These options would waste the personal allowance of the year that the loss was first set against. He could alternatively set the loss against his share of the partnership profits of estimated £30,000 in 2024/25. This would avoid wasting any personal allowance, since his property income exceeds the allowance.
>
> The opening years option of setting the loss against the three tax years before the year of the loss would mean he could set the loss against his property income of 2020/21, followed by 2021/22. This would save minimal amounts of tax and waste the whole personal allowance of 2020/21 and most of the personal allowance for 2021/22.
>
> The recommended most tax-efficient option for Jack would be to carry the loss forward against his share of the partnership profits of 2024/25.

(b)

> Jonah has no other income since he joined the partnership to set his loss against. He could set some of the loss against his £10,000 share of the partnership income of 2022/23, but this is currently covered by his personal allowance, so would not save any tax. He could alternatively set the loss against his share of the partnership profits of estimated £30,000 in 2024/25. However, this would waste most of his personal allowance for that year, since his remaining income would be only £5,000.
>
> The opening year provisions would give Jonah a more tax-efficient option. He could set the loss against his employment income of £50,000 in 2020/21. The whole loss could be used in that year, without wasting the personal allowance. This is the recommended option.

Task 10

(a)

	Capital Gain £
Goodwill	130,000
Buildings	150,000
Plant and machinery	0
Van	0
Net current assets	0
Total gains	280,000
Annual Exempt Amount	6,000
Gain charged at 10%	200,000
Gain charged at 20%	74,000

(b)

	True
The disposal will result in a balancing charge in the main pool for capital allowances	✔
The impact of the disposal on the capital allowances will result in a reduction in trading profits	
Sonia can make no further claims for Business Asset Disposal Relief in the future	✔

Answers to practice assessment 2

Task 1

(a)

	£
Profit	336,875
Disallowed items added back:	
Lisa's salary and personal pension contributions	75,400
Legal fees to purchase new office building	10,250
Operating lease of 180 g/km car used for business	1,749
Expenses of Lisa's car which is used 70% for the business	3,750
Depreciation	155,310
Allowed items deducted:	
Capital allowances	21,380
Adjusted trading profits	561,954

(b) **(a)** and **(b)** Add back to profit; **(c)** No adjustment required; **(d)** Deduct from profit

Task 2

	Full Expensing FYA £	Other FYA £	AIA £	Main Pool £	Special Rate Pool £	Capital Allowances £
Period Ending 31/3/2024						
WDV bf				157,500	31,680	
Acquisition Car 0 g/km		29,500				
100% FYA		(29,500)				29,500
Acquisition Used Machinery			606,000			
AIA 7/12 x £1,000,000			(583,333)			583,333
Trf bal Main pool			(22,667)	22,667		
Sub totals				180,167	31,680	
WDA 18% x 7/12				(18,918)		18,918
WDA 6% x 7/12					(1,109)	1,109
WDV cf				161,249	30,571	
Capital Allowances						632,860
Period Ending 30/6/2024						
Disposal Proceeds				(255,500)	(22,100)	
Disposal Proceeds				(19,800)		
Balancing Allowance					(8,471)	8,471
Balancing Charge				114,051		(114,051)
WDV cf				0	0	
Net Capital (Charge)						(105,580)

Task 3

(a)

To 31 August 2023	Olly £	Pete £
Share of profits	19,200	19,200
From 1 September 2023	**Olly £**	**Pete £**
Interest on capital	875	700
Salary	8,750	7,000
Share of profits	14,574	21,861

(b)

	Profits	Class 4 at 9%	Class 4 at 2%	Total Class 4 NIC
	£	£	£	£
Brian	54,780.00	3,393.00	90.20	3,483.20
Colin	44,820.00	2,902.50	0	2,902.50

Task 4

(a)

	£	£
Proceeds		43,500
Disposal costs		300
Cost	19,850	
Buying costs	650	
Indexation allowance	12,936	
Gain		9,764

(b) If Exe Limited wishes to defer the gain by using rollover relief, the earliest date that qualifying asset(s) can be acquired is **15 January 2023** and the latest is **15 January 2027.**

To obtain deferment of the whole gain, the qualifying asset(s) must cost at least £**1,540,000.**

Task 5

(a)

Date & Details	Number	Cost £	Indexed Cost £
1/1/92 Purchase	5,000	22,500	22,500
1/1/95 Bonus	1,250		
Indexation to 2001 0.279			6,278
1/12/01 Rights	3,125	20,313	20,313
Sub Totals	9,375	42,813	49,091
Indexation to 2017 0.604			29,651
Sub Totals	9,375	42,813	78,742
20/4/23 Disposal	(3,500)	(15,984)	(29,397)
Balance cf	5,875	26,829	49,345

(b)

	£	£
Proceeds		65,000
Cost – April purchase	18,000	
Indexed cost – pool	29,397	
		47,397
Gain		17,603

Task 6

(a)

	First accounting period	Second accounting period
	£	£
Capital gains	5,510	19,475
Trading profits	113,556	47,315
TTP	119,066	66,790

(b)

	First accounting period	Second accounting period
	£	£
Corporation Tax at main rate	22,623	16,698
Less marginal relief		561*
Corporation Tax payable	22,623	16,137

* 3/200 (104,167 – 66,790)

Task 7

(a)

Payment date	Amount
	£
31 July 2023	7,725
31 January 2024	4,800
31 July 2024	6,750

(b) 1 May 2024

(c) **(a)**, **(c)** and **(d)** are False; **(b)**, **(e)** and **(f)** are True

(d)

Minimum £	675
Maximum £	1,350

Task 8

(a)

> Tax evasion is the illegal reduction of tax paid, by, for example, failing to declare taxable income, or claiming fictitious expenses. Tax planning involves using tax legislation as it was originally intended to legally and ethically reduce tax.
>
> Jonathan's suggestion of employing his wife would be considered tax planning. It appears that the salary level being proposed is in line with the work that she carries out for the business, and this would be 'wholly and exclusively' for business purposes.

(b)

> Jonathan is currently subject to Income Tax and Class 2 and Class 4 National Insurance on the profits of the business. The level of his drawings is irrelevant for these purposes.
>
> Since the profits are £70,000, Jonathan would be a higher rate taxpayer, with a marginal tax rate of 40%. Class 2 NIC is a flat rate, but Class 4 NIC would be charged at 9% on profits between £12,570 and £50,270, and 2% on profits above this level.

(c)

> The salary of Sue would be tax-deductible for Jonathan's business, and would save Jonathan Income Tax at his marginal rate of 40%. The salary would be subject to employers' NIC, although the employment allowance could be claimed against this.
>
> Sue would pay Income Tax and employees' NIC on her salary. She would utilise her personal allowance of £12,570 against her employment income, and only pay Income Tax at 20% on the balance. She would pay NIC at 12% on her earnings above £12,570.
>
> A practical issue would be that Jonathan would need to register to operate PAYE on Sue's earnings, and provide monthly data and payments to HMRC.
>
> An alternative to employment would be to form a partnership with Jonathan. A formal agreement would be required, but the split of profits could be agreed in the most beneficial way. Both partners would then be taxed on their share of the profits, and Sue's income would not be tax-deductible by the business.

Task 9

(a)

	£
How much trading loss can be claimed against income in the year ended 31 March 2024?	12,000
How much trading loss can be claimed against income in the year ended 31 March 2023?	29,250
How much trading loss can be carried forward to the year ended 31 March 2025?	0
How much capital loss can be carried forward against capital gains in the year ended 31 March 2025?	5,650
How much QCD can be set against income in the year ended 31 March 2023?	1,800
How much QCD can be set against income in the year ended 31 March 2024?	0
How much QCD can be carried forward to be set against income in the year ended 31 March 2025?	0

(b)

Under the general loss provisions, Chantelle could offset her loss against her total income of 2022/23 and 2023/24. This could be carried out in either order of years. There would be £1,000 income remaining in one of the years after the whole loss was offset.

This would eliminate any Income Tax for both these years, but it would waste the majority of the personal allowances. It would save tax at 20% on up to £21,000 income.

Under the terminal loss provisions, Chantelle could offset her trading loss against the trading income only, working back from 2022/23 for up to three years. In this case, it would eliminate the trading income in 2022/23, and offset £24,000 loss against 2021/22, leaving trading income that year of £2,500. The loss offset would not extend to 2020/21.

This option would leave the personal allowances available against her other income in all years. She would remain a basic rate taxpayer in 2020/21, but would pay minimal tax in 2021/22, and no tax in 2022/23 or 2023/24. This option would save tax at 20% on the whole loss of £45,000, and the terminal loss option is therefore recommended.

Task 10

(a)

	Capital Gain £
Goodwill	50,000
Shop building	330,000
Shop fittings	0
Inventory	0
Total gains	380,000
Annual Exempt Amount	6,000
Taxable Amount	374,000
Capital Gains Tax	37,400

(b)

	True
The disposal will result in a balancing allowance in the main pool for capital allowances	
The impact of the disposal on the capital allowances will result in a reduction in trading profits	
The sale of inventory at cost will not increase Mark's taxable profits	✔

Answers to practice assessment 3

Task 1

(a) **(a)** and **(d)** Deduct from net profit; **(b)**, **(e)** and **(g)** No adjustment required; **(c)** and **(f)** Add back to net profit

(b)

	£
Profit	400,180
Disallowed items added back:	
Operating lease of 180 g/km car	1,479
Replacement of office furniture	12,000
Depreciation	245,110
Allowed items deducted:	
Capital allowances	33,780
Adjusted trading profits	624,989

Task 2

(a)

	Full Expensing FYA £	Other FYA £	AIA £	Main Pool £	Special Rate Pool £	Capital Allowances £
WDV bf				125,000	47,000	
Addition Car 170 g/km					28,000	
Addition Computer*	905,000					
Full Expensing*	(905,000)					905,000
Disposal Proceeds				(5,000)		
Sub Totals				120,000	75,000	
WDA 18% x 8/12				(14,400)		14,400
WDA 6% x 8/12					(3,000)	3,000
WDV cf				105,600	72,000	
Total Capital Allowances						922,400

*Note that full expensing is preferable to AIA here, since AIA would be restricted to £1,000,000 x 8/12 = £666,667.

(b)   (i)

Date	Cost	Amount £	Eligible for SBA
1 April 2022	Purchase of land	560,000	
25 May 2022	Planning permission fees	4,500	
31 August 2022	Factory design fees	65,000	✔
30 September 2022	Site preparation work	155,000	✔
30 January 2023	Construction interim payment	475,000	✔
1 November 2023	Construction final payment	325,000	✔
31 January 2024	Purchase of fixed machinery	175,000	

(ii)   1 December 2023

Task 3

(a)

	Total	Adam	Ben	Clive	Catherine
	£	£	£	£	£
Period to 31 August	150,000	75,000	45,000	30,000	0
Period from 1 September					
Salaries	31,500	14,000	14,000	0	3,500
Share Balance	178,500	59,500	59,500	0	59,500
Total for year	360,000	148,500	118,500	30,000	63,000

(b)

	£
Class 2 NIC	179.40
Class 4 NIC at 9%	3,393.00
Class 4 NIC at 2%	1,364.60

Task 4

	£
Proceeds	1,790,000
Original cost	830,000
Enhancement expenditure	425,000
Indexation on original cost	479,740
Indexation on enhancement expenditure	0
Total gain	55,260
Gain chargeable immediately	0
Gain deferred	55,260
Base cost of warehouse	1,794,740

Task 5

Matching shares bought 20 April 2023	£		
Proceeds (2,000)	9,900		
Cost	9,600		
Gain	300		
Share pool	No	£	£
October 2001 purchase	5,000	15,900	15,900
Bonus shares	500		
Indexation			9,476
Sub total	5,500	15,900	25,376
Disposal	(1,000)	(2,891)	(4,614)
Pool balance	4,500	13,009	20,762
Matching with pool	£		
Proceeds (1,000)	4,950		
Indexed cost	4,614		
Gain	336		
Total gain	636		

Task 6

(a)

	CAP 12 months to 31/7/2023 £	CAP 5 months to 31/12/2023 £
Trading Profits before CAs	504,000	210,000
Capital Allowances	74,000	41,000
Trading Profits	430,000	169,000
Chargeable Gains	0	6,000
Rental Income	37,200	15,500
Sub total	467,200	190,500
QCD	0	6,000
TTP	467,200	184,500

(b)   (i)

£28,987

Working:
Corporation Tax at main rate   £120,000 x 25%   £30,000
Less marginal relief: 3/200 x (£187,500 - £120,000)   (£1,013)
                                                        £28,987

(ii)

£84,600

Working:
FY 2022:   TTP £90,000 x main rate 19%   £17,100
FY 2023   TTP £270,000 x main rate* 25%   £67,500
                                               £84,600

*Limit in FY 2023 for 9 months is £187,500

(iii)

£23,300

Working:
Corporation Tax at main rate   £95,000 x 25%   £23,750
Less marginal relief: 3/200 x (£125,000 - £95,000)   (£ 450)
                                                      £23,300

Task 7

(a)

Payment date	Amount £
31 July 2023	9,200
31 January 2024	13,850
31 July 2024	10,750

(b)   31 May 2024

(c)   **(a)** is False; the remaining statements are True

(d)

Minimum £	14,175
Maximum £	28,350

Task 8

(a)

Tax avoidance and tax evasion

Tax avoidance is the legal use of claims and allowances to reduce the amount of tax payable. Tax evasion involves using illegal methods to reduce tax. There is a grey area between these two activities, and it is not always clear how HMRC or the courts will define a particular activity or scheme.

Where a scheme relies on concealment, pretence, non-disclosure or misrepresentation, this would be categorised as tax evasion which can result in criminal prosecution. 'Aggressive' tax avoidance schemes may also be examined under the recent General Anti-Abuse Rule (GAAR) legislation which will consider whether the law is being used in the way that Parliament originally anticipated.

Implications of joining the scheme

If HMRC is aware of a particular scheme, it does not mean that it has approved it as being legal. There could be ongoing investigations into the scheme which could result in it being declared illegal. Taxpayers must disclose their use of avoidance schemes, and will consequently be viewed as high risk individuals by HMRC. Their tax affairs may be subject to more scrutiny as a result.

Details of other clients

Details of other clients should not be provided as this would be a breach of confidentiality.

Ethical implications for you and your practice

Accountants should also consider their own ethical position when clients wish to undertake tax avoidance, and distance themselves from situations that do not meet their own or their professional body's ethical standards. They must also consider any reputational damage that may occur as a result of facilitating their clients' involvement in particular schemes.

(b) **(i)**

> Both the salary and the employers' NIC are tax-deductible for Corporation Tax purposes. The Corporation Tax will therefore be calculated as:
>
> £75,000 – £47,270 – £5,267 = £22,463 TTP x 19% = £4,268 (small profits rate)
>
> The remaining profits available for dividends would be:
>
> £22,463 – £4,268 = £18,195

(ii)

> Corporation Tax for the company would not be affected by the extraction of profits through dividends, as they are not tax-deductible.
>
> Julian would pay Income Tax at 33.75% on the dividends that he received from his company. This is because the salary and the existing investment dividends use up the personal allowance, the basic rate tax band, and the dividend allowance.
>
> Dividends do not attract employees' or employers' NIC, so there would be no impact on National Insurance.

Task 9

(a) **(i)**

	2022	2023	2024
	£	£	£
Trading profits	120,500	0	375,000
Net chargeable gains	50,300	0	0
Rental income	10,800	12,400	14,200
Trading loss offset against taxable total profits	72,600	12,400	0
Taxable total profits after offsetting losses	109,000	0	389,200

(ii)

> The method outlined in part (i) saves Corporation Tax at 19% (the main rate applicable to FY 2021 and FY 2022). If the loss was offset against the year ended 31 March 2024 it would save Corporation Tax at the main rate of 25% that applies to FY 2023.

(b)

> George could carry the loss forward and set it off against trading income of 2023/24, followed by as many later years as necessary. This would delay any cash flow advantage considerably, although it would probably waste very little personal allowance.
>
> George could set off the loss against his total income of either 2022/23 or 2021/22, or both, in either order. Setting off against 2022/23 would provide minimal tax benefit, and this would also waste the personal allowance for that year.
>
> Setting the loss off against the total income of 2021/22 would enable the whole loss to be set off. The remaining income of £10,000 would be set against the personal allowance, so that no Income Tax would be payable for that year. Any that had been paid already would be refunded. While this option would waste a minority of the personal allowance for that year, the major cash flow advantage means that this is the recommended option.

Task 10

(a)

	Capital Gain £
Goodwill	50,000
Machinery	0
Car	0
Net current assets	0
Total gains	50,000

(b)

Total balancing charge(s)	£70,000

(c)

	True
The calculation of the balancing charge in the main pool for capital allowances will incorporate the disposal proceeds of the car	✔
The reduction in profits due to the balancing charge could result in a terminal loss	

Reference Material

For AAT Assessment of Business Tax

Finance Act 2023

For assessments from 29 January 2024

Note: This reference material is accessible by candidates during their live computer based assessment for Business Tax.

This material was current at the time this book was published, but may be subject to change. Readers are advised to check the AAT website or Osborne Books website for any updates.

Reference material for AAT assessment of Business Tax

Introduction

This document comprises data that you may need to consult during your Business Tax computer-based assessment.

The material can be consulted during the practice and live assessments by using the reference materials section at each task position. It's made available here so you can familiarise yourself with the content before the assessment.

Do not take a print of this document into the exam room with you*.

This document may be changed to reflect periodical updates in the computer-based assessment, so please check you have the most recent version while studying. This version is based on **Finance Act 2023** and is for use in AAT Q2022 assessments from **29 January 2024**

*Unless you need a printed version as part of reasonable adjustments for particular needs, in which case you must discuss this with your tutor at least six weeks before the assessment date.

Note that page numbers refer to those in the original AAT Guidance document

Contents

1. Income tax

Trading allowance			£1,000
Personal allowance			£12,570
	Basic rate (0-£37,700)	Higher rate (£37,701 - £125,140)	Additional rate (Above £125,140)
Salary	20%	40%	45%
Dividends	8.75%	33.75%	39.35%
Trading income	20%	40%	45%

- Income tax computations will not be required in the assessment, but the rates may be used in tax planning discussions.

2. National Insurance (NI)

Class 2 contributions	£3.45 per week
Lower profits threshold	£12,570
Class 4 contributions on trading profits between £12,570 and £50,270	9%
Class 4 contributions on trading profits above £50,270	2%

- Dividends are not subject to NI
- Salaries are subject to:
    - employee NI at 12% between £12,570 and £50,270 and 2% above £50,270
    - employer NI at 13.8% above £9,100 (an employment allowance of £5,000 is available)

    Calculations of NI on salaries will not be required in the assessment but the rates may be used in tax planning discussions

3. Capital gains tax

Annual exempt amount	£6,000
Basic rate	10%
Higher rate	20%
Business asset disposal relief rate	10%
Business asset disposal relief lifetime allowance	£1,000,000

4. Corporation tax

Rate of corporation tax prior to 1 April 2023	19%
Main rate of corporation tax from 1 April 2023	25%
Small profits rate of corporation tax from 1 April 2023	19%
Upper limit	£250,000*
Lower limit	£50,000*
Marginal small company relief	3/200 x (upper limit -TTP)

*reduced if:
- accounting period <12 months
- associated companies.

5. Capital allowances

Assets other than cars:	
Annual investment allowance	£1,000,000
Writing down allowance	18%
Full expensing – expenditure by companies after 1 April 2023	100%

Cars:	
Writing down allowance:	
- CO2 emissions 0g/km	100%
- CO2 emissions up to 50 g/km	18%
- CO2 emissions over 50 g/km	6%

Small pools allowance	£1,000
Structures and buildings allowance	3%

6. Disallowed expenditure

Type of expense	Disallowable in calculation of trading profit	Notes
Fines and penalties	Fines on the business Fines on directors/owners	Employee fines are not disallowed if incurred in the course of their employment.
Donations	Political donations Donations to national charities	Donations to local charities are allowable (these will only be examined for unincorporated businesses).
Capital expenditure	Depreciation Loss on disposal Capital items expensed	Capital allowances may be available.
Legal and professional	Relating to: - capital items - purchase/renewal of a long lease - purchase of a short lease (50 years or less) - breaches of law/regulations.	Legal fees on the renewal of a short lease (50 years or less) are allowable.
Entertaining and gifts	Customer gifts (unless <£50 per annum, not food, drink, tobacco, or cash vouchers and contains business advertising). Customer/supplier entertaining.	Staff gifts and staff entertaining are allowable.
Cars	Depreciation. Private use by owners. 15% of lease cost if leased car >50g/km CO_2 emissions.	
Private expenditure of owner (unincorporated businesses only)	Goods taken for own use. Salary of owners. Private use % by owners. Private expenditure, e.g., Class 2 and 4 NICs, legal and professional fees for personal expenditure.	Reasonable salaries of family members are allowable.

7. Trading losses

Loss option	Sole trader/Partner	Company
Carry forward	Against future profits of the same trade only. Applies automatically to first available profits. Applies after any other elections or if no elections are made.	Losses not relieved in the current accounting period or previous 12 months are carried forward and an election can be made to set against total profits in future periods.
Current year/carry back	Against total income in the current and/or previous tax year in any order. If opted for in either year, the amount of loss used cannot be restricted to preserve the personal allowance. Make claim by 31 January 2026 for 2023/24 tax year.	Can elect to set trading losses against current accounting period 'total profits'. Qualifying charitable donations will remain unrelieved. If the above election is made, can also carry back trading loss to set against 'total profits' within the previous 12 months. Claim within 2 years of the end of the loss-making period.
Opening year loss relief – loss in first four years of trade	Against total income of the previous three tax years on a FIFO basis. If opted for, losses will be used to reduce total income as much as possible in each year and cannot be restricted to preserve the personal allowance. Make claim by 31 January 2026 for 2023/24 tax year.	N/A
Terminal loss relief	Against trading profits of the previous 3 years on a LIFO basis. Claim within 4 years from the end of the last tax year of trade.	Against total profits of the previous 3 years. Claim within 2 years of the end of the loss-making period.

8. Chargeable gains – Reliefs

Relief	Conditions
Replacement of business assets (Rollover) relief	Available to individuals and companies. Examinable for companies. Qualifying assets (original and replacement) – must be used in a trade and be land and buildings or fixed plant and machinery. Qualifying time period – replacement asset must be purchased between one year before and three years after the sale of the original asset. Partial reinvestment – if only some of the sales proceeds reinvested then the gain taxable is the lower of the full gain and the proceeds not reinvested.
Gift relief (holdover relief)	Available to individuals only. Qualifying assets – assets used in the trade of the donor or the donor's personal company, shares in any unquoted trading company or shares in the donors personal trading company. A personal trading company is one where the donor has at least 5%.
Business asset disposal relief	Available to individuals only. Gain taxable at 10%. £1m lifetime limit For 2023/24 a claim must be made by 31 January 2026. Qualifying assets: - the whole or part of a business carried on by the individual (alone or in partnership). The business must have been owned for 24 months prior to sale - assets of the individual's or partnership's trading business that has now ceased. The business must have been owned for 24 months prior to cessation and sale must be within 3 years of cessation - shares in the individual's 'personal trading company' (own at least 5%). The individual must have owned the shares and been an employee of the company for 24 months prior to sale.

9.   Payment and administration

	Sole traders/partners	Company
Filing date	31 October following the end of the tax year if filing a paper return. 31 January following the end of the tax year if filing online. Amendments can be made within 12 months of the filing deadline.	Filed on the later of 12 months after end of AP or 3 months after the notice to deliver a tax return has been issued. Amendments can be made within 12 months of the filing deadline.
Payment date	31 January following the end of the tax year. If payments on accounts are due: • first POA – 31 January during tax year • second POA – 31 July after tax year • balancing payment – 31 January after tax year. POA's are each 50% of the previous years income tax and class 4 NICS due by self-assessment. POA's are not required for capital gains or class 2 NICs. POA's are not due if prior year tax payable by self-assessment is less than £1,000 OR if >80% of prior year tax was collected at source.	Small companies (annual profits less than £1.5 million): 9 months + 1 day after end of the accounting period (AP). Large companies (annual profits greater than £1.5 million) must estimate the year's tax liability and pay 25% of the estimate on the 14th day of each of the 7th, 10th, 13th and 16th month from the start of the accounting period.
Interest	Charged daily on late payment	Interest charged daily on late payment. Overpayment of tax receives interest from HMRC. Interest is taxable/tax allowable as interest income.
Penalties for late filing	£100. After 3 months, £10 per day for up to 90 days. After 6 months, 5% tax due (or £300 if greater). After 12 months, 5% tax due (or £300 if greater) if not deliberate. After 12 months, 70% of tax due (or £300 if greater) if deliberate and not concealed. After 12 months, 100% tax due (or £300 if greater) if deliberate and concealed.	£100. After 3 months, £100. After 6 months, 10% of unpaid tax. After 12 months, 10% of unpaid tax.
Late payment	30 days late – 5% of tax outstanding at that date. 6 months days late – 5% of tax outstanding at that date. 12 months late – 5% of tax outstanding at that date.	N/A

Notify of chargeability	5 October following the end of the tax year.	Within 3 months of starting to trade.
	Sole traders/partners	**Company**
Enquiry	Within 12 months of submission of return. Penalty for failure to produce enquiry documents = £300 + £60 per day.	Within 12 months of submission of return. Penalty for failure to produce enquiry documents: £300 + £60 per day.
Record retention	Five years from filing date. Penalty for failure to keep records is up to £3,000.	Six years after the end of the relevant accounting period. Penalty for failure to keep proper records is up to £3,000.

10. Penalties for incorrect returns

Type of behaviour	Maximum	Unprompted (minimum)	Prompted (minimum
Careless error and inaccuracy are due to failure to take reasonable care	30%	0%	15%
Deliberate error but not concealed	70%	20%	35%
Deliberate error and concealed	100%	30%	50%

for your notes

for your notes

for your notes

for your notes

for your notes

for your notes

for your notes

for your notes

for your notes

for your notes

for your notes

for your notes

for your notes

for your notes

for your notes